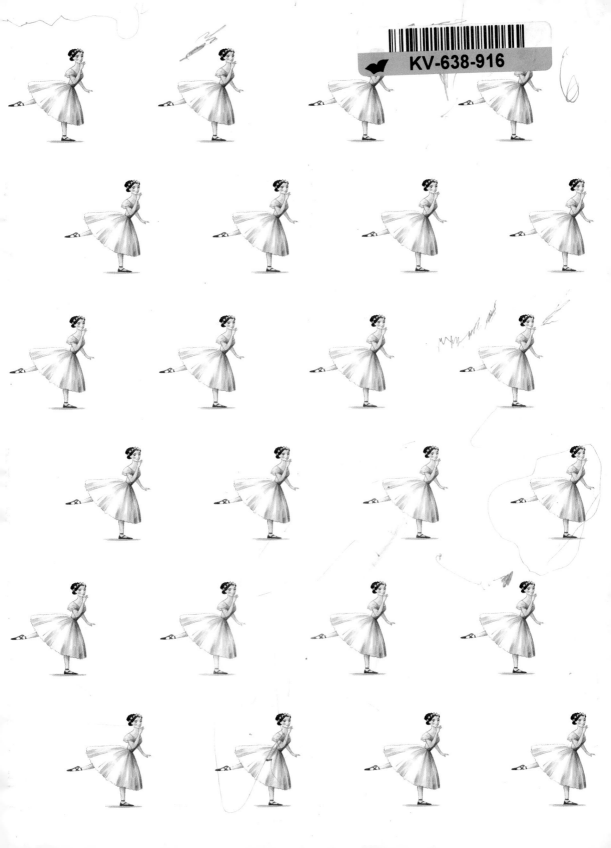

First published in Great Britain in 2000 by
David & Charles Children's Books,
Winchester House, 259-269 Old Marylebone Road, London NW1 5XJ

Text © Adèle Geras 2000
Illustrations © Emma Chichester Clark 2000

ISBN: 1 86233 236 3

Printed and bound in Belgium

The Magic of the Ballet

The Nutcracker

RETOLD BY ADÈLE GERAS
ILLUSTRATED BY EMMA CHICHESTER CLARK

David & Charles
Children's Books

The Magic of the Ballet

HUMAN BEINGS LIKE TO move their bodies in time to rhythm. Even the tiniest babies enjoy being rocked or gently bounced as you sing to them, and we all know how feet long to move when we hear a strong and exciting beat. 'That's toe-tapping music,' we say, and what we mean is we would like to dance to it.

There are many different kinds of dance: folk, disco, ballroom, tap and so on.

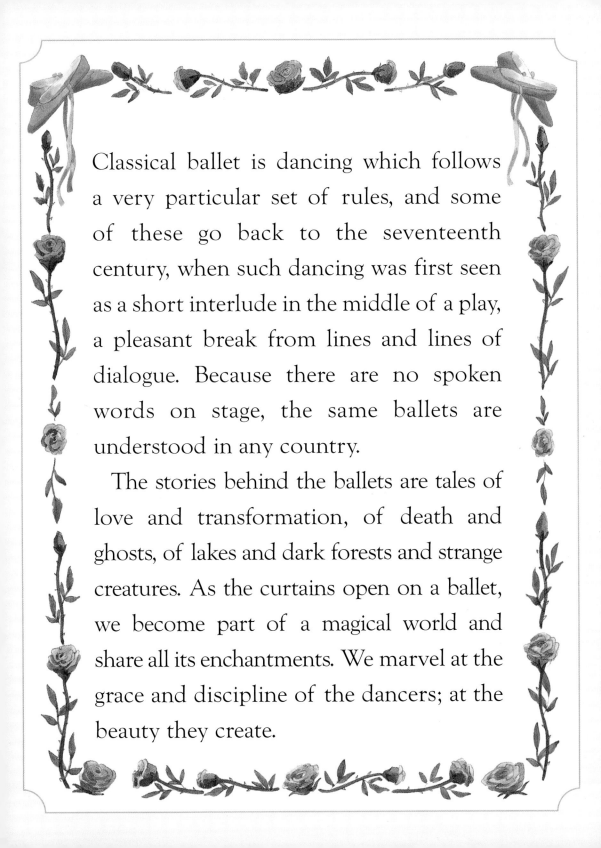

Classical ballet is dancing which follows a very particular set of rules, and some of these go back to the seventeenth century, when such dancing was first seen as a short interlude in the middle of a play, a pleasant break from lines and lines of dialogue. Because there are no spoken words on stage, the same ballets are understood in any country.

The stories behind the ballets are tales of love and transformation, of death and ghosts, of lakes and dark forests and strange creatures. As the curtains open on a ballet, we become part of a magical world and share all its enchantments. We marvel at the grace and discipline of the dancers; at the beauty they create.

'Snowflakes, enormous and intricately patterned,
circled all about us.'

The Nutcracker

"DREAMS," WHISPERED A DISTANT voice in Clara's ear, "are strange and wonderful things, and dreams that are dreamed on Christmas Eve are the strangest and most wonderful of all."

Clara opened her eyes. There was the china cabinet, and the fireplace, and there in the corner was the Christmas tree. This was most definitely the parlour. Why was she lying on the scratchy plush of the sofa? Why was she not in her own bed, waking up to look for her stocking full of nuts and oranges and twists of golden barley sugar? Clara turned her head and caught sight of the present Dr Drosselmeyer had given her last night at the party: a wooden nutcracker in the shape of a man. Clara picked him up and cuddled him.

"I love you best, Nutcracker," she said. "Better than my dolls. Better than any game. Better than all my other presents. Do you remember being in my dream last night? Do you remember how it all started? I do."

Clara sat up and gathered the travelling rug more closely round her shoulders.

"Now I shall tell you the whole story, Nutcracker," Clara said. "Sit comfortably on this cushion and I'll go right back to the beginning of our party."

The nutcracker said nothing, but he seemed content to listen, so Clara continued. "We always have a party, every year on Christmas Eve. Everyone comes to it: grandfathers and grandmothers, aunts, uncles, cousins, friends and neighbours and Dr Drosselmeyer. Dr Drosselmeyer is not a relation and he's not really a friend but he always comes to the house on Christmas Eve and brings the most marvellous presents.

The preparations for the party were almost as exciting as the party itself. All day long, the house had been full of the most mouth-watering smells, and at last Mama began to set out the food on the long table.

'If you children help with the cakes and sweets,' Mama said, 'there will be none left for the guests! Go instead and fetch your Papa and decorate the tree.'

That's what we did, Nutcracker, and oh, when we'd finished, it was the most beautiful Christmas tree in the whole world. We tied red ribbons on the branches. We hung up painted pine cones, and gingerbread biscuits iced in pink and white, and chocolate coins in glittery paper, and Papa found a silver star for the very top of the tree.

As for the food, you cannot imagine how delicious it was. There were cinnamon biscuits and golden shortbread and animals made out of marzipan. There were tiny crystallised fruits, and sugared almonds and salted almonds, and every cake you can think of: ginger cakes and chocolate ones, and apple cakes and sponges, all set out on dainty china plates patterned with flowers, ivy leaves and trailing ribbons.

The snow started falling at about four o'clock. Fritz and I watched it from our nursery window as it fell from the dark sky, dancing and whirling as the wind lifted it and

tossed it over the rooftops, but always in the end falling and falling until everything we could see was covered in white.

'Just like the icing on one of the cakes downstairs,' said Fritz.

When the guests came into the house, snowflakes came in with them: on their hats and capes, on their gloves and boots, and they shook them off, laughing.

'Dr Drosselmeyer is here!' Fritz cried and we both went into the hall to greet him.

'Good evening, children,' he said in his gravelly voice. 'Come and see who I have brought to your party.'

Standing behind him in the shadows were a pretty young lady and a young man wearing a harlequin costume.

'I have taken the liberty of inviting the real Harlequin and Columbine to the festivities.' He put a skinny finger to his lips and whispered to us, 'They are dancing dolls, my

dears, nothing more. Lifesize and very convincing, but only dolls, when all is said and done. Let us see if we can play a trick on the grown-ups.'

And they believed him, Nutcracker. Everyone believed him. Harlequin and Columbine danced for all the guests, and everyone thought they were real. When the dance was over and the secret a secret no longer, all the children clustered round the dolls, touching their stiff limbs that only a moment ago had been so full of life and movement.

Then, Dr Drosselmeyer gave us our presents. There was a set of soldiers in a wooden box for Fritz and you were my gift. Oh, I was delighted with you, and everyone admired you greatly. During the parlour games and dances, I never let you out of my sight, and when Fritz and the other boys took you and began cracking nuts with you, why, I nearly burst into tears. I did cry when they broke you. Anyone would have. How could they have given you such an enormous nut? It would have broken the strongest nutcracker in the world. Dr Drosselmeyer noticed my tears.

'Do not cry, Clara. This is a prince among nutcrackers, and see, a twist here and a turn there and he is as good as new.' The doctor's bony, white hands moved so fast that I could not see what he did, but you were quite mended when he returned you to me.

The end of a party is a sad time, Nutcracker, isn't it? All the candles on the

tree had burned out, the gingerbread biscuits were all eaten, the table had been cleared and the white lace cloth folded away. Fritz had put his soldiers back into their box, and I had put you here, on the sofa cushions, to rest until morning. But I couldn't sleep. The thought of you, all alone in the dark parlour, kept me awake. I thought: I will creep down and sit on the sofa and keep my Nutcracker company for a while.

The room was in darkness, except for a faint glow from the embers in the fireplace. I tiptoed to the sofa and sat holding you in my hand. From a long way away, I heard the town clock chiming midnight. Suddenly, the Christmas tree, standing like a shadow in the corner, began to grow. It grew and grew, up and up towards the ceiling with a rustling and creaking and sighing of the branches, and as it grew, the candles seemed to be alight once again, and in a few moments, the tree was towering high, high above my head. Now I know I must have been dreaming, but last night I thought there was a special Christmas magic in the air, for all at once, you and I were the same size and I didn't even stop to consider how strange this was. Then, in the silence of the night, we heard a scratching and a squeaking from behind the Christmas tree.

'It's the Army of Mice,' you said. Yes, you could speak and it seemed to me altogether normal that you should. 'They have come to do battle with the toy soldiers.'

I could hardly believe my eyes. The mice and the soldiers were enormous. They were the same size as we were, and some were even larger. Our Turkish carpet was turned into a battlefield, with Fritz's army waving their swords and shooting their cannons and marching towards their enemy.

You, my brave Nutcracker, decided to attack the Mouse King, a fearsome iron-grey

creature with glittering red eyes.

'Nutcracker!' I cried, afraid. 'He will break you . . . I cannot let you be broken again!'

Suddenly, I was no longer frightened. Instead, I was filled with anger. I took off my slippers and threw them, as hard as I could, at the Mouse King. Perhaps I was helped by Christmas magic once more, for both slippers hit the Mouse King full in the face. He was not expecting slippers to come flying through the air, and he ran away squealing into the shadows under the sideboard. His Mouse Army followed him and soon the soldiers were marching triumphantly back to their box.

'Thank you, Clara,' you said to me. 'You saved my life.'

When I turned to look at you, you were no longer made of wood. You had become a real person, living and breathing . . . a handsome prince. Then you took my hand and we came to sit together on this sofa.

'Your kindness deserves a reward,' you said. 'Close your eyes and do not open them until I tell you to.'

I closed my eyes and felt the sofa moving. It seemed to me that I was flying up and up. I could feel a breeze around us, but I wasn't cold, in spite of being dressed only in my nightgown.

'Open your eyes, Clara,' you said to me. 'We are in the Land of Snowflakes.'

There was nothing in the Land of Snowflakes but clear, dark blue everywhere: above, below and all around us. The sofa was floating on it, through the velvety night. Snowflakes,

enormous and intricately patterned, circled all about us like white moths, floating and drifting, falling and turning.

'They are dancing, Clara,' you told me. 'They are dancing a Snowflake Waltz.'

And indeed, when I looked at them more closely, I could see that this was so. Round and round they twirled, like pretty ladies in white dresses, round and round to a music that grew out of the blue night and swelled around us.

'Come,' you said, when the last snowflake had blown away. 'Now it is time to go somewhere altogether warmer.'

'Where?' I asked. 'Where are we going now?'

'To a party in the Land of Sweets.'

'I have never heard of such a land. When will we reach it?'

'Soon,' you answered. 'Soon. We must hurry. The Sugar Plum Fairy is waiting for us in her palace.'

Now everyone has heard of the witch's house in the story of Hansel and Gretel – the one that was made of things to eat – and I think I was expecting something like that. But I could not have imagined anything half as splendid as the palace of the Sugar Plum Fairy. It was gigantic, and made entirely of pink sugar, spun into domes and turrets and battlements. It was set in a garden full of caramels, marzipan rosebushes, nut-cakes, raisins and pistachios, arranged in tubs and in flowerbeds. The sentries were silver-coated chocolate soldiers.

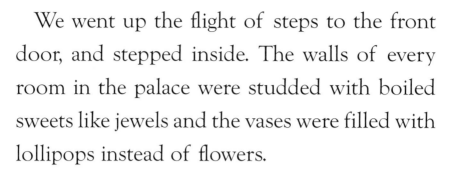

We went up the flight of steps to the front door, and stepped inside. The walls of every room in the palace were studded with boiled sweets like jewels and the vases were filled with lollipops instead of flowers.

Then, the Sugar Plum Fairy appeared.

'Welcome, Prince Nutcracker, and welcome, Clara, to the Land of Sweets. All that is delicious is waiting for you here.'

Her pink dress caught the light as though she had been sprinkled from head to toe with grains of the finest sugar.

'When you have eaten and drunk, my

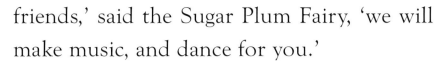

friends,' said the Sugar Plum Fairy, 'we will make music, and dance for you.'

The lamps were lit, and fountains sprang to life. Do you remember all the dances, Nutcracker? There was one in honour of chocolate, with all the dancers in Spanish costumes, then one for coffee, with the dancers dressed in veils and richly-patterned Arabian robes. And did you notice the dragons embroidered on the jackets of the Chinese dancers, who represented tea? Oh, they were magnificent. Then came the Russian dancers, with high leather boots and fur hats, and dancers pretending to be reed flutes, and best of all was a huge old lady with a wide, wide skirt under which were hidden dozens and dozens of children.

'Who's that?' I asked, and the Sugar Plum Fairy answered, 'She has many names. Some people call her Mother Ginger or Mother Marshmallow, or even the Old Woman who

Lived in a Shoe, but I call her Mère Gigogne.'

Mère Gigogne and her children stepped aside, the Waltz of the Flowers began, and then, do you remember, Nutcracker? You danced with the Sugar Plum Fairy. To me it seemed as though her feet never touched the ground. You looked so beautiful, both of you. I have never seen a lovelier sight.

There's always a dance at the end of every party, but in the Land of Sweets the last waltz was like a kaleidoscope of sparkling colours, turning and turning.

After the party was over, you and I, Nutcracker, went back into the garden of the palace, and sat down again on our sofa.

'It is time for you to leave us,' said the Sugar Plum Fairy as she bent to kiss me goodbye. 'Take a little rose from this marzipan rosebush.' She put into my hand a pink flower nestling among leaves of green angelica.

'Thank you,' I said. 'It has been like a dream.'

'Dreams,' said the Sugar Plum Fairy, 'are strange and wonderful things, and the dreams that are dreamed on Christmas Eve are the strangest and most wonderful of all.'

That's what she said to me, Nutcracker. Then I woke up. There was a rug covering me. Mama must have come in and found me asleep. Wasn't that a lovely dream, Nutcracker?"

Clara listened for the nutcracker's answer, but he only smiled and said nothing.

Unnoticed under the sofa, a small pink marzipan rose, nestling among green angelica leaves, lay where it had fallen.

THE NUTCRACKER WAS PERFORMED for the first time in 1892. It was choreographed first by Petipa and then by Lev Ivanov after Petipa fell ill. The story is by Hoffmann, and the music was the last great ballet score written by Tchaikovsky before his death.

You can dance to any music as long as it has a strong, definite rhythm. There have been ballets set to jazz, rock'n'roll, and many classical pieces that were not written especially for the dance. For example, the ballet, *Les Sylphides* can also be called *Chopiniana* because Fokine choreographed it as a physical embodiment of music of Chopin.

Sometimes the composer tries to express a story, or a

scene that the choreographer has visualized. Tchaikovsky was supremely skilled at doing this, and so was Stravinsky, who wrote the score for *The Firebird*. Prokofiev is another famous composer whose *Romeo and Juliet* is still performed by every major ballet company. There is a beautiful version of it on video, danced by Rudolf Nureyev and Margot Fonteyn.

Music written for ballet has to do some of the same things as film music. It has to help to convey a certain atmosphere. It tells us the mood we are supposed to be in. If you listen to ballet music with your eyes closed, you will know which bits are frightening or happy; which are soothing and dreamy; and which remind you of a grand occasion. When composing *Romeo and Juliet*, Prokofiev used each note and bar to convey a sense of unease, longing and forboding. Initially, each movement sounds beautifully and delicately woven, though if you listen carefully, you will hear a series of contrasting notes that fit awkwardly with the rest of the piece. Prokofiev realised that the listener would detect these subtle hints intended to reflect the mood of the story, and would become unsettled by them. So successful was this method that Leonard Bernstein mirrored it when writing the score for *West Side Story*, itself a modern day version of *Romeo and Juliet* set on the streets of New York.

Some ballet music is so well-known that we associate it with other things. Advertisers have often used ballet music in their jingles and ballet music is frequently played in school for such things as walking into and out of assembly. It comes as a delightful surprise when you see your first ballet and recognize a melody you know already transformed by being a part of a beautiful whole. Music does far more than provide a background for the dancing. It is the transformation of what the composer has written into what we hear that casts the first spell. The music is where the magic begins.

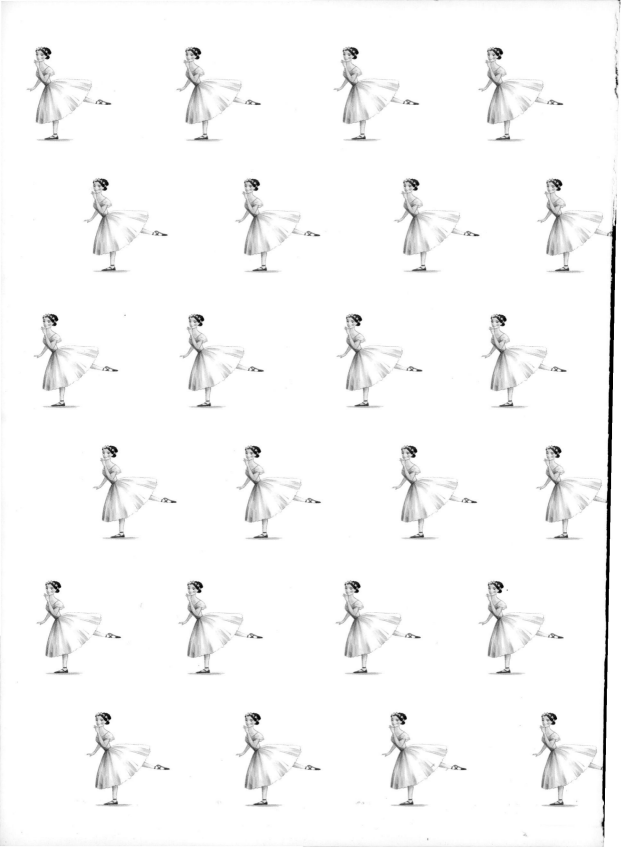